Everybody Digs Soil

DIFFERENT KINDS OF SOIL

Molly Aloian

Crabtree Publishing Company

www.crabtreebooks.com

Crabtree Publishing Company

www.crabtreebooks.com

Author: Molly Aloian

Editor-in-Chief: Lionel Bender

Editor: Lynn Peppas

Project coordinator: Kathy Middleton

Photo research: Susannah Jayes

Designer: Ben White

Production coordinator: Ken Wright

Production: Kim Richardson

Prepress technician: Ken Wright

Consultant: Heather L. Montgomery, children's writer, environmental educator, and science education consultant who runs Dragonfly Programs: http://www.dragonflyeeprograms.com

Cover: Most plants cannot grow in sand because it holds few nutrients.

Title page: Planting a tree sapling

This book was produced for Crabtree Publishing Company by Bender Richardson White.

Photographs and reproductions:

© BigStockPhoto.com: pages 11 right (Phil Morley), 15 left (Marcin Radtke), 19 bottom (Brendan Montgomery)

Dreamstime: cover (bottom soil)

© Getty Images: pages 10 (Ryan Mcvay), 11 left (Inga Spence), 16 (Jim Dyson), 18 (Image Source),

© iStockphoto.com: Headline image (redmal), title page and pages 28/29 (Pattie Calfy), 4 (Clayton Hansen), left(Perdix), 6/7 (jcgsees), 9 left (Michael Fernahl), 12 (Natalia Bratslavsky), 13 top (Terry Patton), 14 (NicolasMcComber), 15 right (Andriy Bezuglov), 17 top (Rafik El Raheb), 17 bottom (Romulus Hossu), 20 bottom (Michael Wicks), 21 (Dan Brandenburg), 22 (Missing35mm), 23 bottom (Dan Eckert), 23 top (Nathaniel Frey), 24/25 top (Brian Raisbeck), 24/25 bottom (Andreas Fischer), 25 (Eli Franssens), 26 (Dan Kite), 27 left (Mike Clarke), 27 right (Windzepher), 29 top (Dean Turner), 29 bottom (Eli Franssens)

Stockbyte/Jupiterimages: cover (girls)

© www.shutterstock.com: cover (bottom soil), pages 5 right (Gravicapa), 7 right, 8 (jacglad) 9 right (Rob Huntley), 13 bottom (Joe Gough), 20 top (Inacio Pires)

USDA Natural Resources Conservation Service: pages 6 left, 19 top

Library and Archives Canada Cataloguing in Publication

Aloian, Molly

    Different kinds of soil / Molly Aloian.

(Everybody digs soil)

Includes index.

ISBN 978-0-7787-5400-8 (bound).--ISBN 978-0-7787-5413-8 (pbk.)

    1. Soils--Juvenile literature. 2. Soil chemistry--Juvenile literature.

I. Title. II. Series: Everybody digs soil

S591.3.A46 2010   j631.4   C2009-906271-2

Library of Congress Cataloging-in-Publication Data

Aloian, Molly.

  Different kinds of soil / Molly Aloian.

    p. cm. -- (Everybody digs soil)

  Includes index.

  ISBN 978-0-7787-5413-8 (pbk. : alk. paper) -- ISBN 978-0-7787-5400-8 (reinforced library binding : alk. paper)

  1. Soils--Juvenile literature. 2. Soil chemistry--Juvenile literature. I. Title. II. Series: Everybody digs soil.

  S591.3.A36 2009

  631.4--dc22

                      2009042779

Crabtree Publishing Company

www.crabtreebooks.com   1-800-387-7650

Printed in the U.S.A./122009/BG20090930

Published in Canada
Crabtree Publishing
616 Welland Ave.
St. Catharines, Ontario
L2M 5V6

Published in the United States
Crabtree Publishing
PMB 59051
350 Fifth Avenue, 59th Floor
New York, New York 10118

Published in the United Kingdom
Crabtree Publishing
Maritime House
Basin Road North, Hove
BN41 1WR

Published in Australia
Crabtree Publishing
386 Mt. Alexander Rd.
Ascot Vale (Melbourne)
VIC 3032

CONTENTS

What is Soil?   4

Layers of Soil   6

Soil Chemistry   8

Humus   10

Textures and Types   12

Sandy Soil   14

Silty Soil   16

Clay Soil   18

Ages of Soil   20

Soil and Climate   22

Soil and Nature   24

Soil and People   26

Caring for Soil   28

Glossary   30

More Information   31

Index   32

WHAT IS SOIL?

A long with water and air, soil is one of the most important natural resources on Earth. Plants, many animals, and tiny **organisms**, or living things, such as bacteria and algae live in soil. Farmers grow crops in soil. Without soil, there would be limited life on Earth.

LIVING SOIL

Soil is the layer of material on Earth's surface. It is under your feet when you walk through the back yard. It gets under your nails when you dig for worms and sticks to your knees when you kneel in the yard. Soil is sometimes called dirt. But soil is alive, dirt is not. Soil is an important part of nature.

▶ *A handful of soil*

SOIL INGREDIENTS

Soil is made up of **biotic** and **abiotic** material: "Biotic" means from living things and "abiotic" from non-living matter. Biotic material includes plants and animals such as earthworms and their waste, and bits of dead plants and animals. Abiotic material is water, air, and bits of rock of different sizes and shapes. "Organic" is a word for biotic material that can be broken down by living things, which is important for soil. It includes dead leaves and stems.

▼ *Plants growing in soil are food for farm animals such as cows, pigs, and sheep.*

▲ *A slice through soil shows grass growing on the surface and roots below.*

LAYERS OF SOIL

Soil can be just a few inches or several feet deep. Either way, soil is different from top to bottom—it is divided into layers called horizons.

TOPSOIL

The first layer of soil is called **topsoil**. It is usually dark, crumbly, and spongy. It contains decaying plant and animal matter called **humus**. Topsoil is also called the "litter zone" as it is full of tree litter—fallen leaves.

A LIVING LAYER

Topsoil is usually very **fertile**, which means that plants grow well in it. There is air and water between the **particles** of topsoil. There are many living things in topsoil.

▶ You can grow your own vegetables and flowering plants in the topsoil of your back yard.

▼ *Digging through soil layers*

SUBSOIL

Subsoil is the second layer of soil. It is light in color because it contains less humus. The weight of the topsoil above presses the soil particles here closer together. As a result, there is less space for water and air. There are fewer living things found in subsoil.

PARENT MATERIAL

Going down, the third soil layer is called **parent material**. This layer contains very little humus. It is made up of rocks, gravel, sand, and clay, the matter from which the layers above are made. Parent material is more pressed down so there is even less water and air in this layer and few living things.

SOIL FACTS

✳ Soil contains **nutrients**. Nutrients are chemicals living things need to survive and grow. Plants take up these nutrients through their root systems.

BEDROCK AT THE BOTTOM

✳ **Bedrock** is the fourth layer of soil. It is solid rock. There are no living things in this layer.

▶ *Soil layers are clear to see in a landslide.*

SOIL CHEMISTRY

Some types of soil are acidic. Other types of soil are **basic**. These words describe a soil's chemistry.

ACIDIC OR BASIC

An acid is a sharp-tasting **chemical**. Some acids can attack metal. Lemon juice is a weak acid. A base is similar but chemically opposite. Washing soda is a strong base. Scientists measure the strength of an acid or base by its **pH** value— a measure of its hydrogen (H) activity. Acids have a low pH, bases a high pH. The pH scale ranges from 0 to 14. The pH of soil varies a lot and is measured in many ways. The pH of soil is important because some plants grow best in a narrow pH range.

Blueberries and a few types of flowers grow best when the soil pH is 5.5 or less—quite acidic. Most garden vegetable plants, shrubs, trees, and lawn grass grow best when the soil pH is more than 6.0 or 6.5. The range between 5.5 and 7.5 is ideal for two main reasons. First, it allows microscopic organisms to break down organic, or living, matter. Second, it allows the most soil nutrients to be released to plants.

▼ *Blueberry bush*

CAUSES AND EFFECTS

What creates acidic or basic soil? Acid rain can turn soil acidic (lower its pH). The rain forms from acids thrown into the air by factory chimneys and car exhaust. Heavy rainfall can naturally wash away some chemicals, leaving soil acidic. Pine needles and pine bark fallen from pine trees also make soil acidic. Rain seeping from chalk and limestone rocks, which are rich in bases, can make the soil basic (raise its pH).

SOIL FACTS

✳ Desert soil tends to be basic. Cactus plants grow best in this kind of soil. Desert soil contains many **minerals**, such as calcium and salt, which cacti use.

▼ *Cacti can survive in hot, dry conditions. Their thick stems store water drawn up from the soil through their roots.*

▲ *These trees have been damaged by acid rain. Acid rain can seriously damage the chemistry of soil.*

HUMUS

If you walk into a forest, you will be walking on humus. Humus is an important part of soil.

DEAD PLANTS AND ANIMALS

Humus is the partly **decomposed**, or broken down, organic matter in soil. It forms from animal waste and dead plant and animal material. It is produced by two main types of micro life, or tiny organisms, in soil: **microbes** and **fungi**. Microbes are tiny organisms that can be seen only through a microscope. They include bacteria and **protozoa**, which are tiny animals. Fungi are living things that live on dead or rotting organic matter. There can be billions of microbes in just a small bit of soil.

Humus is rich in leaf, bark, and twig material. It has a black or dark brown color because it contains a lot of the chemical carbon.

NOURISHING NUTRIENTS

Humus contains nutrients including nitrogen, phosphorus, potassium, calcium, and magnesium. Nitrogen helps plants grow and stay green. Phosphorus helps plants grow flowers, fruits, roots, and seeds. Potassium helps plants fight diseases. Calcium helps plants take up other nutrients they need and helps roots and leaves grow. Magnesium helps plants during **photosynthesis**, the process of making their own food.

▶ *Leaf litter*

▶ *Humus is the layer of soil with the most wildlife, especially worms.*

TEXTURES AND TYPES

Many scientists sort, or name, soils based on the amount of sand, silt, or clay they contain. Different amounts of sand, silt, or clay make a range of soil textures and types.

SAND, SILT, OR CLAY

Particles are tiny pieces of something. Sand is made of large particles or grains. Silt has smaller particles. Clay has very small particles. Sandy soil has a lot of sand in it so it feels gritty. It is often light in color. Silty soil feels smooth and usually has a brownish color. Clay soils feel slippery and sticky and usually have a dark brown color.

FOREST SOIL

The soil in a forest contains silt. This provides nutrients that help trees, other plants, and micro life stay alive. Insects, bacteria, fungi, and algae usually live in the top two feet (60 cm) of forest soil. Silt also traps rainwater that runs off trees, preventing the soil from drying out. Finally, silt filters, or takes out, various minerals and **impurities** from the water before it enters streams and rivers. This keeps river water clean and healthy.

▼ *Deep in a forest*

GRASSLAND SOIL

Grassland soil is dark and silty but often contains a lot of clay. It is rich in humus so many grasses grow in it. Grass roots grow as much as six feet (1.8 m) into the ground. This helps hold the soil in place. The roots prevent the soil from **eroding**, or wearing away, in strong winds and heavy rains.

PRAIRIE DOGS

Prairie dogs dig underground homes, called burrows, in soil. The digging creates air pockets in the soil. Other soil-dwelling animals need this air to survive. The burrows also fill with rainwater, which waters the soil.

▼ *A prairie dog*

SOIL FACTS

✳ The soil in tropical rain forests is not fertile because all the nutrients are stored in the lush trees and other plants. In most tropical rain forests, the topsoil is only one to two inches (2.5 to 5 cm) deep.

SANDY SOIL

Have you ever stuck your feet into wet sandy soil on a beach? Do you remember the texture of the sand— neither smooth nor rough? If you visit a pebble beach, you will see rocks on their way to becoming sand.

SAND SITUATION

Sandy soil has a lot of sand in it. The extra sand allows water to drain through it, so sandy soil dries out quickly after rain. Sandy soil is made up of particles that are smaller than gravel, but larger than silt. Sandy soil contains little organic material.

▼ *On the beach*

SAND FACTS

* Grains of sand are the largest soil particles, but they are still tiny. They usually measure between 0.0024 inches (0.06 mm) and 0.08 inches (2.0 mm) across.

* Sea water tumbles cliff rocks together until they break apart into smaller and smaller pieces. Eventually, the rocks turn into sand.

* Most plants cannot grow in sandy soil because it holds few nutrients. A few plants, such as cacti, thrive in sandy soil.

▼ *Sand grains magnified*

COLORED SAND

Sandy soil can sometimes be colorful. The sand in Bermuda is coral-colored. It is made of limestone, coral, and pieces of shells. Soil from Hawaii is mostly black. It is made with sand from crumbled and eroded lava, the hot, molten rock thrown out by volcanoes.

▶ *Playing with wet sand*

15

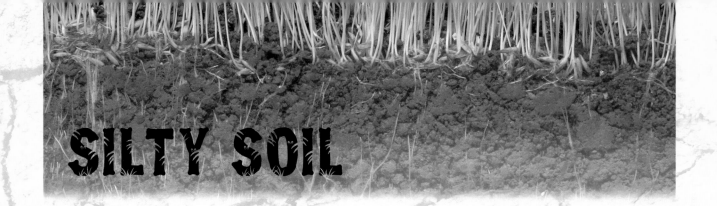

SILTY SOIL

Have you ever made mud pies? Have you ever put a mud mask on your face? If you answered "yes," then you have felt silt on your fingers.

SMOOTH AS SILT

Silty soils feel smooth and powdery. They can hold a lot of water and often have a brownish color. Silt is made mainly of the mineral called quartz. Silt is found in soil, but it can also be found floating as sediment, or tiny grains, in a lake or pond. Silt is sometimes washed up on land by flooding rivers or lakes. Some rivers, such as the Nile River in Egypt, carry a lot of silt. Others carry only a little silt. Crops grow well in silty soil because it is rich in nutrients and holds water for a long time.

▶ Silt often feels sticky. It can certainly stick to shoes and clothes!

SPREADING SILT

In Egypt, farmers rely on flooding of the Nile River to improve the soil. Each year, the river floods and overflows onto its banks. The flooding spreads nutrient-rich silt over the desert. It also brings water than can be piped in channels to distant land. Farmers grow many crops, or food plants, in the silty soil.

▲ *Farmland between the Nile River and desert hills*

YOU DIG IT

Examine grains of sand and silt with a magnifying glass. Look at particles of clay under a microscope. How do they look?

SILT FACTS

✳ Silt particles are smaller than sand particles, but larger than clay particles. Grains of silt usually measure between 0.00016 inches (0.004 mm) and 0.0024 inches (0.06 mm).

✳ Silt is sometimes called "rock flour" or "stone dust" because its grains are so fine.

◀ *Silt can collect on roofs and form soil. Plants grow and trap warmth in the house.*

CLAY SOIL

Have you ever used clay to make different shapes? How many shapes did you make? How did the clay feel in your hands?

SLIMY CLAY SOILS

Clay soils feel slippery and slimy. They can hold large amounts of water, but become very hard when completely dried out. These soils usually have a dark brown or gray color. But clay can be many other colors, including deep orange-red. Clay soils are formed over long periods of time as rocks become **weathered**, or dissolved by water. They are rich in nutrients including calcium, potassium, and magnesium.

◄ A potter takes a lump of wet clay, spins it on a wheel, then shapes it into a vase. He will place the vase in an oven to bake the clay until hard.

NOT ENOUGH WATER

Many trees and shrubs grow well in clay soils. In thick clay soils, however, the roots of most flowering and vegetable plants are not strong enough to make their way through. Also, clay soil does not release enough water for these plants to use. Finally, air cannot **circulate**, or flow around, plant roots in many clay soils.

YOU DIG IT

Mix some water with a handful of soil and try to determine if the soil is mostly sand, silt, or clay. With your fingers, rub the clumps of soil to break them up.

CLAY FACTS

✳ "Quick clay" changes easily from a solid lump to liquid. It is involved in deadly landslides.

✳ Clay particles are the smallest soil particles. You can see them only with a microscope because they are smaller than 0.00016 inches (0.004 mm) across.

◀ *A tractor pulls a plow through soil to break it up and allow air and water in.*

AGES OF SOIL

▲ Lichen on a rock

HOW IS SOIL MADE?

Young or new soil is formed when wind and water cause rocks to break down into tiny pieces. Changes in temperature also cause rocks to expand and contract, then crumble. Plants such as lichens and mosses root themselves in the cracks and crevices of the rocks. As these roots grow, they cause rocks to break down into ever smaller pieces. This is how new soil forms. But new soil cannot support many plants and animals because it is mostly rock and has little biotic matter.

Soil forms slowly. It can take about 500 years for just one inch (2.5 cm) of soil to build up. Some soils may be many thousands of years old.

▲ *Soil must be mature, or well aged, before trees and shrubs can grow.*

GROWING UP

As soil ages, it becomes more fertile. Nutrients that are taken in by plants and animals are returned back to the soil as other plants and animals die and **decompose**. Mature, or old, soil is ideal for growing crops and can support many plants because it has a thick layer of humus.

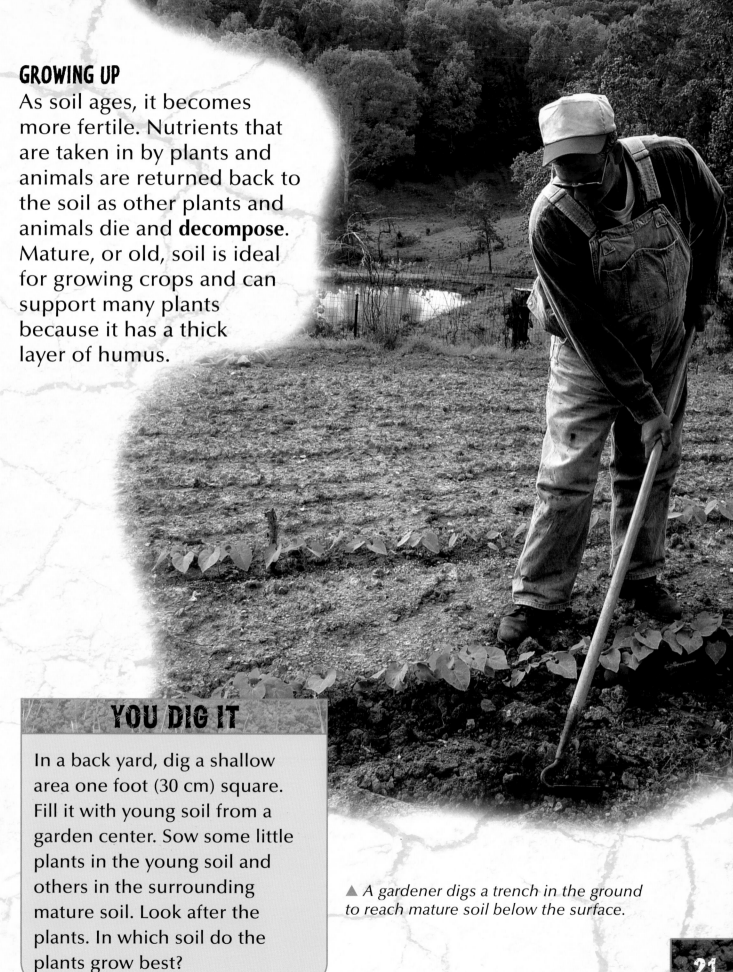

YOU DIG IT

In a back yard, dig a shallow area one foot (30 cm) square. Fill it with young soil from a garden center. Sow some little plants in the young soil and others in the surrounding mature soil. Look after the plants. In which soil do the plants grow best?

▲ A gardener digs a trench in the ground to reach mature soil below the surface.

21

SOIL AND CLIMATE

Different parts of the world have different climates or general weather conditions. The climate in an area affects soil in a variety of ways.

TEMPERATE AND TROPICAL SOIL

Soil often contains more organic matter in places with **temperate**, or warm and damp, climates. This makes it fertile. Trees, grasses, and other plants grow well in these soils. In tropical places, the heat and rain allow soil to form quickly. But tropical soils do not contain a lot of nutrients and can be very acidic. They are not always fertile. Farmers can grow crops in tropical soils for only one or two years before all the nutrients disappear.

TUNDRA SOIL

The climate is cold in the Arctic tundra. The soils here are wet and soggy. Water remains on the surface of the soil because the lower layers of soil are permanently frozen. Mosses, lichens, and sedges are among the few plants that grow in tundra soils. Organic matter does not break down very easily in cold climates.

▼ *Tundra landscape*

DESERT SOIL

There are hot deserts such as the Sahara. The polar regions are cold deserts. All deserts receive less than 10 inches (25 cm) of rain each year. In hot deserts, the soil is often sandy and gritty and is not very fertile.

▼ *Cacti roots do not grow down far because desert soils are thin. Their roots do grow outward for many feet.*

BLOWING AWAY

Desert soils can easily be blown away because they contain hardly any water. Different types of cacti and brittle bush grow in hot, sandy desert soil. In cold deserts, any soil is covered in snow and ice, and it is too cold for most living things to survive.

SOIL FACTS

✳ During the "Dust Bowl" of the 1930s, much of the soil of the prairies was blown away, ruining farms.

▼ *Desert foxes on the hunt for food*

23

SOIL AND NATURE

Soil plays an important role in Earth's **ecology** and life cycles. It supports plant and animal life. Millions of living things make their homes in soil.

A RANGE OF SIZES

Cells are the microscopic building bricks of living things. Tiny soil organisms, such as bacteria and protozoa, are made of just one cell. Bigger organisms have many cells. These include algae, mosses, and such fungi as mushrooms and toadstools. All these living things create or release nutrients into soil, allowing plants to grow. Big animals eat these plants or one another. This "food chain" depends on the important role soil plays in nature.

▶ *Flowers produce seeds that, in ideal soil conditions, make new plants.*

SOIL FACT

✳ Scientists began studying soil in the late 1700s. The science of studying soil as a natural resource is called pedology.

24

YOU DIG IT

Add a package of colored drink mix to water. Shake the mixture and then filter it through different kinds of soil. What happens? Which type of soil is most affected?

DECOMPOSING ORGANIC MATTER

Spiders and insects, including ants, beetles, and many kinds of bugs, help break down the organic matter in soil. As these animals dig through soil, they create pathways so air and water get into the soil. Earthworms are one of the most important animals that live in soil. They eat organic material then dump undigested food on the surface as "casts" or coils of soil. In doing this, they bring fertile soil to the top.

◄ *Plants take nutrients from the soil. Plant-eaters, such as buffalo, take up the nutrients. Meat-eaters, such as lions, take in the nutrients from the animals they eat. When lions die or get rid of waste, they return nutrients to the soil.*

KEEPING CLEAN

Soil absorbs, or sucks up, water. All living things need water to stay alive. Soil also helps keep the water supply clean. It traps pollutants, or unwanted or harmful chemicals, before they **leach,** or seep, into the ground and then into rivers, ponds, and lakes.

► *A lake with clear water*

SOIL AND PEOPLE

BUILDING MATERIALS

People build homes, schools, and other structures on soil. In some parts of the world, people make buildings and houses from mud bricks. They mix soil with water, straw, and animal waste and shape the mixture into bricks. After the bricks harden, people use them to make homes. Adobe homes are made of bricks made with mud, straw, and grasses.

People need soil to survive. Soil has always played a part in human life. Try to think of all the ways people use and rely on soil.

IT ALL BEGINS WITH SOIL

Vegetables, fruits, eggs, meat, wood, and building materials all have their beginnings in soil. Fruits and vegetables come from plants grown in soil. Livestock eat plants that grow in soil. Wood comes from trees, and mud and straw are the materials needed to make certain types of bricks. During photosynthesis, plants release **oxygen**. Most living things, including people, need oxygen to survive.

◀ A mud brick mosque, or place of worship, in Mali, Africa

IN THE PAST

The tough remains of plants and animals that lived millions of years ago have been preserved in mud. These **fossils** form in soil that has hardened to become solid rock. Fossils can be different shapes and sizes, but often only parts of the plant or animal are fossilized. Scientists are interested in fossils because they provide information about life on Earth long ago.

SOIL FACT

✳ Cement is made from clay, sand, and gravel. It is used to make concrete roads, sidewalks, and buildings.

◀ Pouring concrete at a construction site

▲ The fossilized remains of an extinct Saber Tooth Tiger

CARING FOR SOIL

More than one-fifth of all the soil on Earth is damaged. Soil is being destroyed at a faster rate than it is being created. Fertile soil takes hundreds of years to create, but it can be damaged or poisoned in just a couple of growing seasons.

▼ Planting trees holds soil in place, adds nutrients, and provides organic matter that will one day create humus.

NO SOIL?

Without healthy soil, farmers cannot grow crops. There would be no trees or other plants, and living things would not have enough oxygen to survive. Soil can be damaged by many things, including **fertilizers**, pollution, pesticides, and **herbicides**. These are chemicals some farmers use to add nutrients or kill plant pests or weeds.

SOIL FACTS

✳ Soil helps control temperatures on Earth. The heat and moisture trapped in soil affects the temperature of land. In turn, this affects rainfall, snowfall, and melting of the ice caps in polar regions. So looking after soil plays a part in keeping global warming in check.

▼ Rainforest landscape

RAIN FORESTS

When large areas of rain forests are not cut down for wood or farmland, the rich soil that has taken many thousands of years to mature is protected.

SOIL PROTECTION

Some people protect soil by allowing houses to be built only on sites that are not ideal for farming. This helps ensure that there is enough healthy soil for growing food. Farmers are also trying out a new kind of farming called **sustainable agriculture**. This allows crops to be grown year after year without harming the soil.

NATURAL IS BEST

"Organic farming" uses natural ways of making soil fertile, keeping soil creatures healthy, and stopping erosion. For example, some farmers use natural killers of pests rather than chemicals.

▲ Vegetables grown organically are packed with nature's nutrients.

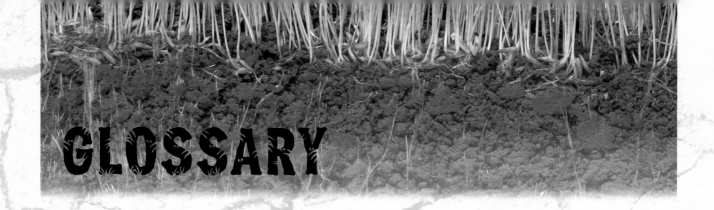

GLOSSARY

acidic Something with a low pH

bacteria Single-celled organisms that break down organic matter

basic Something with a high pH

cell The basic unit of all living things

chemical A natural substance, such as carbon, oxygen, hydrogen or nitrogen

circulate To always move in a circle

climate The general weather conditions

decompose To break down into chemicals

ecology The links between living things and their environment

eroding Wearing away growing plants

fertile Good for growing plants

fertilizers Chemicals added to soil to give it more nutrients

fossils The remains of a plant or animal from long ago that is preserved in soil or rock

herbicides Chemicals added to soil to kill unwanted plants

impurities Unwanted substances in a mix

leach To pass a liquid through something

mineral Any useful chemical such as salts or some metals

organisms Living things

oxygen A gas found in air that living things need to stay alive

particles Very small parts of matter. Soil is a mix of particles

pH A number used to measure how strong an acid or base a substance is. pH values range from 0 to 14.

photosynthesis The way plants make food from simple chemicals using the energy of sunlight

protozoa Tiny single-celled animals

silt Fine grains of rock

sustainable agriculture Farming without damaging soil, water, or air

temperate Climate that is warm and damp

weathered Changed by exposure to weather

MORE INFORMATION

FURTHER READING

Minerals, Rocks, and Soil. Davis, Barbara. Sci-Hi, 2009.

The Nature and Properties of Soils. Brady, Nyle C. and Weil, Raymond C. Prentice Hall, 2007.

Dirt: The Ecstatic Skin of the Earth. Logan, William Bryant. W.W. Norton, 2007.

Life in a Bucket of Soil. Silverstein, Alvin. Dover Publications, 2000.

I Love Dirt! Ward, Jennifer. Trumpeter, 2008.

Sand and Soil: Earth's Building Blocks. Gurney, Beth. Crabtree Publishing Company, 2005

WEB SITES

Soil for Schools:
www.soil-net.com/legacy/schools/index.htm

Discovery Education—The Dirt on Soil:
http://school.discoveryeducation.com/schooladventures/soil/

Buzzle.com Latest Articles—Soil Types, Soil Conservation:
www.buzzle.com/articles/different-types-of-soil.html
www.buzzle.com/articles/10-ways-to-conserve-soil.html

INDEX

abiotic 5
acidic 8, 9, 22
air 4, 5, 6, 7, 11, 13,
    19, 25
algae 4, 12, 24
animals 4, 5, 6, 10, 13,
    20, 21, 24, 25, 27

back yard 4, 6, 21
bacteria 4, 10, 12, 24
basic 8, 9
bedrock 7
biotic 5, 20, 21
building materials 26
burrows 13

cacti 9, 15, 23
calcium 11, 18
cell 24
chemistry 8–9
clay 7, 11, 12, 13, 17,
    18–19, 27
climate 22–23
color 12, 15, 16, 18

decaying matter 6, 10,
    25
deserts 5, 9, 17, 23
drainage 14

earthworms 4, 5, 11, 25
erosion 13, 15, 29

farm animals 5, 26
farmers and farming
    4, 16, 17, 21, 22, 23,
    28, 29

fertile 6, 13, 21, 22, 23,
    25, 28, 29
food chain 24
forests 5, 10, 12, 13
fossils 27
fungi 10, 12, 24

global warming 28
grassland 13

humus 6, 7, 10–11, 13,
    21, 28

ingredients 5
insects 12, 25

lakes and ponds 5,
    16, 25
layers 4, 6–7, 11, 22
leaves 5, 6, 10, 11
lichens 20, 22
loam 11
looking after 28–29

magnesium 11, 18
micro life 10, 12
microbes 10
minerals 9, 12, 16
mosses 20, 22, 24

nitrogen 11
nutrients 7, 8, 11, 12,
    15, 16, 17, 18, 21, 22,
    24, 25, 28, 29

organic matter 5, 8, 10,
    11, 14, 20, 22, 25, 28

parent material 7
particles 6, 7, 11, 12,
    14, 15, 17, 19
pH value 8, 9
phosphorus 11
photosynthesis 11, 26
plants 4, 5, 6, 7, 8, 10,
    11, 12, 13, 15, 17, 19,
    20, 21, 22, 24, 25, 26,
    27, 28
potassium 11, 18
protozoa 10, 24

rain 9, 13, 22, 28
rivers 5, 12, 16, 17, 25
rock 5, 7, 9, 11, 14, 15,
    17, 18, 20, 27
roots 5, 7, 9, 11, 13, 19,
    20, 23

sand 7, 11, 12, 14, 15,
    17, 19, 23, 27
silt 11, 12, 13, 14,
    16–17, 19
subsoil 7

textures 12–13, 14, 18
topsoil 6, 13
trees 6, 8, 9, 12, 13, 19,
    20, 22, 26, 28
types 12–13

waste 5, 9, 10, 26
water 4, 5, 6, 7, 11, 12,
    13, 14, 15, 16, 17, 18,
    19, 20, 22, 23, 25, 26
weathering 18